CUTE & COZY
Sweaters and Blankets

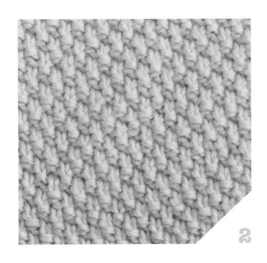

2

8

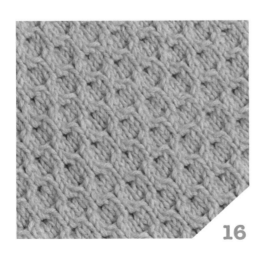

16

22

For gifts that will bring smiles to the faces of Mom and Baby, knit these stylish cardigans in light weight yarn. The cozy matching blankets are worked with double strands of the same yarn.

LEISURE ARTS, INC. • Maumelle, Arkansas

SOFT TOUCH SWEATER

Size: 6 months

Finished Chest Measurement: 19" (48.5 cm)

■■■□ INTERMEDIATE

SHOPPING LIST

Yarn (Light Weight)

[5 ounces, 362 yards
(140 grams, 331 meters) per skein]:

☐ 1 skein

Knitting Needles

29" (73.5 cm) Circular,

☐ Size 4 (3.5 mm) **and**

☐ Size 5 (3.75 mm)

  or sizes needed for gauge

Straight,

☐ Size 4 (3.5 mm) **and**

☐ Size 5 (3.75 mm)

  or sizes needed for gauge

Additional Supplies

☐ Point protectors - 2

☐ Stitch holders - 3

☐ Tapestry needle

☐ Sewing needle

☐ Sewing thread

☐ ⁹⁄₁₆" (14 mm) buttons - 3

GAUGE INFORMATION

With larger size straight needles,
  in Body pattern,
  24 sts and 32 rows = 4" (10 cm)

TECHNIQUES USED

- YO *(Fig. 1, page 30)*
- Knit increase *(Figs. 2a & b, page 30)*
- K2 tog *(Fig. 4, page 30)*
- SSK *(Figs. 6a-c, page 30)*
- P2 tog *(Fig. 8, page 31)*

BAND

Sweater is worked in one piece to underarms.

With smaller size circular needle, cast on 120 sts.

Rows 1-9: Knit across.
Row 10: K5, knit increase, K8, knit increase, (K9, knit increase) 9 times, K8, knit increase, K6: 132 sts.

BODY

Change to larger size circular needle.

Row 1 (Right side)**:** K7, P1, (K1, P1) across to last 6 sts, K6.
Row 2: P6, K1, (P1, K1) across to last 7 sts, P7.
Rows 3 and 4: P7, K1, (P1, K1) across to last 6 sts, P6.
Rows 5 and 6: K7, P1, (K1, P1) across to last 6 sts, K6.
Row 7: K6, P1, (K1, P1) across to last 7 sts, K7.
Row 8: P7, K1, (P1, K1) across to last 6 sts, P6.
Rows 9 and 10: P6, K1, (P1, K1) across to last 7 sts, P7.
Rows 11 and 12: K6, P1, (K1, P1) across to last 7 sts, K7.
Rows 13-51: Repeat Rows 1-12, 3 times; then repeat Rows 1-3 once **more**.

Row 52: P5, P2 tog, K8, P2 tog, (K9, P2 tog) 9 times, K8, P2 tog, P6: 120 sts.

Dividing Row: K3, **[YO, K2 tog (buttonhole made)]**, K 23 (Right Front), bind off next 6 sts (Armhole), K 51 (Back), bind off next 6 sts (Armhole), knit across (Left Front): 28 sts on each Front and 52 sts on Back.

LEFT FRONT
ARMHOLE SHAPING

Row 1: Using larger size straight needles, K6, purl across Left Front, leave remaining sts on circular needle and place point protectors on each end to keep sts from slipping off needle while working Left Front: 28 sts.

Row 2: K1, SSK, knit across: 27 sts.

Row 3: Purl across.

Row 4: K1, SSK, knit across to last 6 sts, P6: 26 sts.

Row 5: Purl across.

Row 6: K1, SSK, knit across: 25 sts.

Row 7: K6, purl across.

Row 8: Knit across.

Row 9: Purl across.

3

Row 10: Knit across to last 6 sts, P6.

Row 11: Purl across.

Row 12: Knit across.

Rows 13-19: Repeat Rows 7-12 once, then repeat Row 7 once **more**.

NECK SHAPING

Row 1: K 16, slip last 9 sts onto st holder: 16 sts.

Row 2: Purl across.

Row 3 (Decrease row): Knit across to last 3 sts, K2 tog, K1: 15 sts.

Row 4: Purl across.

Rows 5-12: Repeat Rows 3 and 4, 4 times: 11 sts.

Bind off remaining sts in **knit**, leaving a long end for sewing.

BACK

ARMHOLE SHAPING

Row 1: With **wrong** facing and using larger size straight needles, purl across Back, leave remaining sts on circular needle and place point protector on end to keep sts from slipping off needle while working Back: 52 sts.

Row 2 (Decrease row)**:** K1, SSK, knit across to last 3 sts, K2 tog, K1: 50 sts.

Row 3: Purl across.

Rows 4-6: Repeat Rows 2 and 3 once, then repeat Row 2 once **more**: 46 sts.

Work even until Back measures same as Left Front, ending by working a **purl** row.

Last 2 Rows: Bind off 11 sts, work across: 24 sts.

Slip remaining sts onto st holder.

RIGHT FRONT

ARMHOLE SHAPING

Row 1: With **wrong** side facing and using larger size straight needles, purl across to last 5 sts, K5: 28 sts.

Row 2: Knit across to last 3 sts, K2 tog, K1: 27 sts.

Row 3: Purl across.

Row 4: P6, knit across to last 3 sts, K2 tog, K1: 26 sts.

Row 5: Purl across.

Row 6: Knit across to last 3 sts, K2 tog, K1: 25 sts.

Row 7: Purl across to last 6 sts, K6.

Row 8: Knit across.

Row 9: Purl across.

Row 10: P6, knit across.

Row 11: Purl across.

Row 12 (Buttonhole row)**:** K3, [YO, K2 tog (**buttonhole made**)], knit across.

Rows 13-17: Repeat Rows 7-11.

Row 18: Knit across.

Row 19: Purl across to last 6 sts, K6.

NECK SHAPING

Row 1: K9, slip 9 sts just worked onto st holder, knit across: 16 sts.

Row 2: Purl across.

Row 3 (Decrease row)**:** K1, SSK, knit across: 15 sts.

Row 4: Purl across.

Rows 5-12: Repeat Rows 3 and 4, 4 times: 11 sts.

Bind off remaining sts in **knit**, leaving a long end for sewing.

SLEEVE (Make 2)
BAND

With smaller size straight needles, cast on 32 sts.

Rows 1-7: Knit across.

Row 8: Knit increase, knit across to last st, knit increase: 34 sts.

BODY

Change to larger size straight needles.

Beginning with a **purl** row, work in Stockinette Stitch, increasing one stitch at **each** edge in same manner, every tenth row twice, then increase every twelfth row once: 40 sts.

Work even until Sleeve measures approximately 6" (15 cm) from cast on edge, ending by working a **purl** row.

CAP SHAPING

Rows 1 and 2: Bind off 3 sts, work across: 34 sts.

Row 3 (Decrease row)**:** K1, SSK, knit across to last 3 sts, K2 tog, K1: 32 sts.

Row 4: Purl across.

Rows 5-9: Repeat Rows 3 and 4 twice, then repeat Row 3 once **more**: 26 sts.

Row 10: Purl across.

Row 11: Knit across.

Row 12: Purl across.

Row 13 (Decrease row)**:** K1, SSK, knit across to last 3 sts, K2 tog, K1: 24 sts.

Rows 14-26: Repeat Rows 10-13, 3 times; then repeat Row 10 once **more**: 18 sts.

Rows 27 and 28: Bind off 4 sts, work across: 10 sts.

Bind off remaining sts in **knit**.

FINISHING

Sew shoulder seams.

COLLAR

With **wrong** side facing and using larger size straight needles, purl 9 sts from Left Front st holder, pick up 11 sts evenly spaced along Left Front neck edge *(Fig. 10, page 31)*, purl 24 sts from Back st holder, pick up 11 sts evenly spaced along Right Front neck edge, slip 9 sts from Right Front st holder onto empty needle and purl across: 64 sts.

Row 1 (Buttonhole row)**:** K3, **[**YO, K2 tog **(buttonhole made)]**, K1, purl across to last 6 sts, K6.

Row 2: P6, K1, knit increase, (K2, knit increase) across to last 8 sts, K1, knit increase, P6: 82 sts.

Row 3: Bind off 6 sts in **purl**, K2, purl across: 76 sts.

Row 4: Bind off 6 sts in **knit**, knit across: 70 sts.

Row 5: K3, purl across to last 3 sts, K3.

Row 6: K2, knit increase, K1, (knit increase, K2) across to last 6 sts, knit increase, K1, knit increase, K3: 93 sts.

Row 7: K3, purl across to last 3 sts, K3.

Row 8: K4, P1, (K1, P1) across to last 4 sts, K4.

Rows 9 and 10: K3, P1, (K1, P1) across to last 3 sts, K3.

Rows 11 and 12: K4, P1, (K1, P1) across to last 4 sts, K4.

Rows 13-16: Repeat Rows 9-12.

Rows 17-19: Knit across.

Bind off all sts in **knit**.

Weave Sleeve seams *(Fig. 11, page 31)*.

Sew Sleeves to Sweater, placing center of last row on Sleeve Cap at shoulder seam and matching bound off stitches.

Sew buttons to Left Front opposite buttonholes.

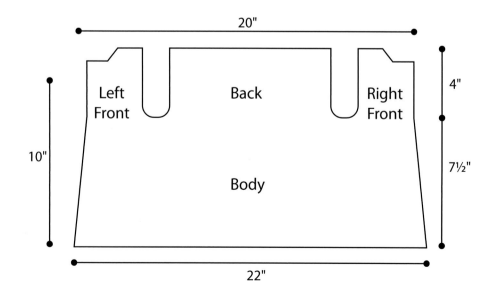

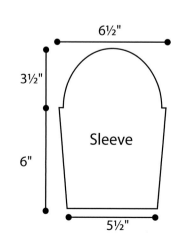

SOFT TOUCH BLANKET

SHOPPING LIST

Yarn (Light Weight)

[5 ounces, 362 yards
(140 grams, 331 meters) per skein]:

☐ 5 skeins

Knitting Needles

29" (73.5 cm) Circular,

☐ Size 5 (3.75 mm) **and**

☐ Size 7 (4.5 mm)

or sizes needed for gauge

GAUGE INFORMATION

With larger size needle,
in Body pattern and
holding two strands
of yarn together,
18 sts and 24 rows = 4" (10 cm)

BOTTOM BORDER

With smaller size needle and holding
two strands of yarn together,
cast on 140 sts.

Rows 1-10: Knit across.

BODY

Change to larger size needle.

Row 1 (Right side)**:** K9, P1, (K1, P1)
across to last 8 sts, K8.
Row 2: K9, P1, (K1, P1) across to last
8 sts, K8.
Rows 3 and 4: K8, P1, (K1, P1) across
to last 9 sts, K9.
Rows 5 and 6: K9, P1, (K1, P1) across
to last 8 sts, K8.

Repeat Rows 3-6 for pattern until
piece measures approximately 39"
(99 cm) from cast on edge, ending by
working Row 4 or 6.

TOP BORDER

Change to smaller size needle.

Rows 1-10: Knit across.

Bind off all sts in **knit**.

TIMELESS SWEATER

Size: 6 months

Finished Chest Measurement:
21½" (54.5 cm)

▣▢▢▢ INTERMEDIATE

SHOPPING LIST

Yarn (Light Weight)
Peach Set
[5 ounces, 459 yards
(140 grams, 420 meters) per skein]:
☐ 1 skein
Blue Set
[1.75 ounces, 161 yards
(50 grams, 147 meters) per skein]:
☐ 3 skeins

Knitting Needles

29" (73.5 cm) Circular,
☐ Size 4 (3.5 mm) **and**
☐ Size 5 (3.75 mm)
   or sizes needed for gauge
Straight,
☐ Size 4 (3.5 mm) **and**
☐ Size 5 (3.75 mm)
   or sizes needed for gauge

Additional Supplies

☐ Point protectors - 2
☐ Stitch holders - 3
☐ Tapestry needle
☐ Sewing needle
☐ Sewing thread
☐ ⅝" (16 mm) buttons - 5

GAUGE INFORMATION

With larger size straight needles,
   in Body pattern,
   24 sts = 4¼" (10.75 cm);
   32 rows = 4" (10 cm)

TECHNIQUES USED

- YO (**Fig. 1, page 30**)
- Knit increase (**Figs. 2a & b, page 30**)
- Purl increase (**Fig. 3, page 30**)
- K2 tog (**Fig. 4, page 30**)
- K2 tog tbl (**Fig. 5, page 30**)
- SSK (**Figs. 6a-c, page 30**)
- Slip 2, K1, P2SSO (**Fig. 7, page 31**)

RIBBING

Sweater is worked in one piece to
underarms.

With smaller size circular needle,
cast on 117 sts.

Row 1: P1, (K1, P1) across.
Row 2: K1, (P1, K1) across.
Rows 3-7: Repeat Rows 1 and 2
twice, then repeat Row 1 once **more**.

BODY

Change to larger size circular needle.

Row 1 (Right side)**:** K2, K2 tog, YO, K1,
YO, K2 tog tbl, ★ K1, K2 tog, YO, K1,
YO, K2 tog tbl; repeat from ★ across
to last 2 sts, K2.
Row 2: Purl across.
Row 3: K1, K2 tog, YO, K3, ★ YO,
slip 2, K1, P2SSO, YO, K3; repeat from
★ across to last 3 sts, YO, K2 tog tbl,
K1.
Row 4: Purl across.
Row 5: K2, YO, K2 tog tbl, K1, K2 tog,
★ YO, K1, YO, K2 tog tbl, K1, K2 tog;
repeat from ★ across to last 2 sts, YO,
K2.
Row 6: Purl across.
Row 7: K3, YO, slip 2, K1, P2SSO,
★ YO, K3, YO, slip 2, K1, P2SSO; repeat
from ★ across to last 3 sts, YO, K3.
Row 8: Purl across.

Repeat Rows 1-8 for pattern until
piece measures approximately 7"
(18 cm) from cast on edge, ending by
working Row 8.

Dividing Row: K2, K2 tog, YO, K1, YO, K2 tog tbl, (K1, K2 tog, YO, K1, YO, K2 tog tbl) 3 times (Right Front), bind off next 5 sts (Armhole), (K1, K2 tog, YO, K1, YO, K2 tog tbl) 9 times, K2 (Back), bind off next 4 sts, K2 tog, pass first st on right needle over second st (Armhole), YO, K1, YO, K2 tog tbl, (K1, K2 tog, YO, K1, YO, K2 tog tbl) 3 times, K2 (Left Front): 25 sts on **each** Front and 57 sts on Back.

LEFT FRONT

Row 1: Using larger size straight needles, purl across Left Front, leave remaining sts on circular needle and place point protectors on each end to keep sts from slipping off needle while working Left Front: 25 sts.

Row 2: K4, ★ YO, slip 2, K1, P2SSO, YO, K3; repeat from ★ 2 times **more**, YO, K2 tog tbl, K1.

Row 3: Purl across.

Row 4: K3, K2 tog, ★ YO, K1, YO, K2 tog tbl, K1, K2 tog; repeat from ★ 2 times **more**, YO, K2.

Row 5: Purl across.

Row 6: K1, ★ YO, slip 2, K1, P2SSO, YO, K3; repeat from ★ across.

Row 7: Purl across.

Row 8: K2 tog, YO, K1, YO, K2 tog tbl, ★ K1, K2 tog, YO, K1, YO, K2 tog tbl; repeat from ★ 2 times **more**, K2.

Row 9: Purl across.

Rows 10-23: Repeat Rows 2-9 once, then repeat Rows 2-7 once **more**.

NECK SHAPING

Row 1: ★ K2 tog, YO, K1, YO, K2 tog tbl, K1; repeat from ★ 2 times **more**, slip last 7 sts onto st holder: 18 sts.

Row 2: Purl across.

Row 3: K4, YO, slip 2, K1, P2SSO, YO, K3, YO, slip 2, K1, P2SSO, YO, K2, SSK, K1: 17 sts.

Row 4: Purl across.

Row 5: K3, K2 tog, YO, K1, YO, K2 tog tbl, K1, K2 tog, YO, K1, YO, K2 tog tbl, K2 tog, K1: 16 sts.

Row 6: Purl across.

Row 7: K1, ★ YO, slip 2, K1, P2SSO, YO, K3; repeat from ★ once **more**, K2 tog, K1: 15 sts.

Row 8: Purl across.

Bind off all sts in **knit**, leaving a long end for sewing.

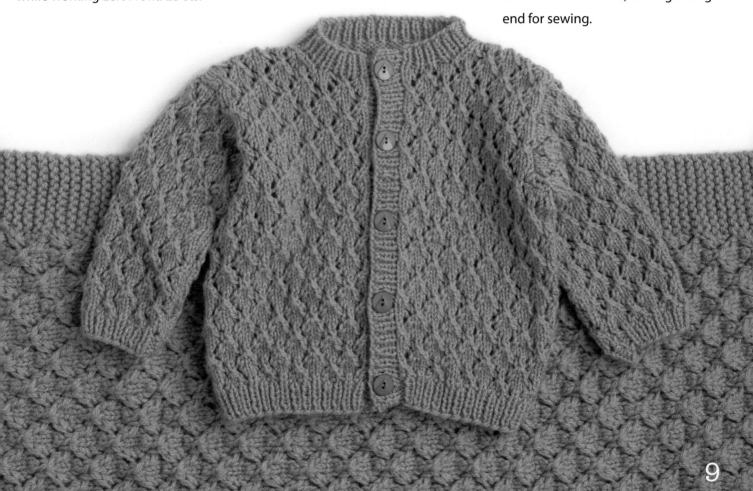

9

BACK

Row 1: With **wrong** side facing and using larger size straight needles, purl across Back, leave remaining sts on circular needle and place point protector on end to keep sts from slipping off needle while working Back.

Row 2: K1, K2 tog, YO, K3, ★ YO, slip 2, K1, P2SSO, YO, K3; repeat from ★ across to last 3 sts, YO, K2 tog tbl, K1.

Row 3: Purl across.

Row 4: K2, YO, K2 tog tbl, K1, K2 tog, ★ YO, K1, YO, K2 tog tbl, K1, K2 tog; repeat from ★ across to last 2 sts, YO, K2.

Row 5: Purl across.

Row 6: K3, ★ YO, slip 2, K1, P2SSO, YO, K3; repeat from ★ across.

Row 7: Purl across.

Row 8: K2, K2 tog, YO, K1, YO, K2 tog tbl, ★ K1, K2 tog, YO, K1, YO, K2 tog tbl; repeat from ★ across to last 2 sts, K2.

Row 9: Purl across.

Rows 10-31: Repeat Rows 2-9 twice, then repeat Rows 2-7 once **more**.

Row 32: Bind off 15 sts, knit across: 42 sts.

Row 33: Bind off 15 sts, purl across: 27 sts.

Slip remaining sts onto st holder.

RIGHT FRONT

Row 1: With **wrong** side facing and using larger size straight needles, purl across: 25 sts.

Row 2: K1, K2 tog, ★ YO, K3, YO, slip 2, K1, P2SSO; repeat from ★ 2 times **more**, YO, K4.

Row 3: Purl across.

Row 4: K2, YO, K2 tog tbl, ★ K1, K2 tog, YO, K1, YO, K2 tog tbl; repeat from ★ 2 times **more**, K3.

Row 5: Purl across.

Row 6: K3, YO, slip 2, K1, P2SSO, ★ YO, K3, YO, slip 2, K1, P2SSO; repeat from ★ 2 times **more**, YO, K1.

Row 7: Purl across.

Row 8: K2, K2 tog, YO, K1, YO, K2 tog tbl, ★ K1, K2 tog, YO, K1, YO, K2 tog tbl; repeat from ★ across.

Row 9: Purl across.

Rows 10-23: Repeat Rows 2-9 once, then repeat Rows 2-7 once **more**.

NECK SHAPING

Row 1: K7, slip 7 sts just worked onto st holder, ★ K1, K2 tog, YO, K1, YO, K2 tog tbl; repeat from ★ across: 18 sts.

Row 2: Purl across.

Row 3: K1, SSK, K2, YO, slip 2, K1, P2SSO, YO, K3, YO, slip 2, K1, P2SSO, YO, K4: 17 sts.

Row 4: Purl across.

Row 5: K1, SSK, K2 tog, YO, K1, YO, K2 tog tbl, K1, K2 tog, YO, K1, YO, K2 tog tbl, K3: 16 sts.

Row 6: Purl across.

Row 7: K1, SSK, ★ K3, YO, slip 2, K1, P2SSO, YO; repeat from ★ once **more**, K1: 15 sts.

Row 8: Purl across.

Bind off remaining sts in **knit**, leaving a long end for sewing.

SLEEVE (Make 2)
RIBBING

With smaller size straight needles, cast on 35 sts.

Row 1: P1, (K1, P1) across.

Row 2: K1, (P1, K1) across.

Rows 3 and 4: Repeat Rows 1 and 2.

Row 5 (Increase Row): Purl increase, K1, (P1, K1) across to last st, purl increase: 37 sts.

BODY

Change to larger size straight needles.

Row 1 (Right side): K1, ★ K2 tog, YO, K1, YO, K2 tog tbl, K1; repeat from ★ across.

Row 2 AND ALL WRONG SIDE ROWS: Purl across.

Row 3: K5, YO, slip 2, K1, P2SSO, ★ YO, K3, YO, slip 2, K1, P2SSO; repeat from ★ across to last 5 sts, YO, K5.

Row 5: K1, ★ YO, K2 tog tbl, K1, K2 tog, YO, K1; repeat from ★ across.

Row 7: K2, YO, slip 2, K1, P2SSO, ★ YO, K3, YO, slip 2, K1, P2SSO; repeat from ★ across to last 2 sts, YO, K2.

Row 9 (Increase row): Knit increase, K2 tog, YO, K1, YO, K2 tog tbl, ★ K1, K2 tog, YO, K1, YO, K2 tog tbl; repeat from ★ across to last st, knit increase: 39 sts.

Row 11: K6, YO, slip 2, K1, P2SSO, ★ YO, K3, YO, slip 2, K1, P2SSO; repeat from ★ across to last 6 sts, YO, K6.

Row 13: K2, YO, K2 tog tbl, K1, K2 tog, ★ YO, K1, YO, K2 tog tbl, K1, K2 tog; repeat from ★ across to last 2 sts, YO, K2.

Row 15: K3, ★ YO, slip 2, K1, P2SSO, YO, K3; repeat from ★ across.

Row 17 (Increase row): Knit increase, K1, ★ K2 tog, YO, K1, YO, K2 tog tbl, K1; repeat from ★ across to last st, knit increase: 41 sts.

Maintaining established pattern, continue to increase one stitch at **each** edge, every eighth row, 2 times **more**: 45 sts.

Work even until Sleeve measures approximately 6½" (16.5 cm) from cast on edge, ending by working a **purl** row.

Bind off all sts in **knit**.

FINISHING

Sew shoulder seams.

NECK BAND

With **right** side facing and using smaller size straight needles, knit 7 sts from Right Front st holder, pick up 7 sts evenly spaced along Right Front neck edge *(Fig. 10, page 31)*, slip 27 sts from Back st holder onto empty needle and knit across, pick up 7 sts evenly spaced along Left Front neck edge, slip 7 sts from Left Front st holder onto empty needle and knit across: 55 sts.

Row 1: K1, (P1, K1) across.
Row 2: P1, (K1, P1) across.
Rows 3-6: Repeat Rows 2 and 3 twice.

Bind off all sts in ribbing.

BUTTONHOLE BAND

Boy's: With **right** side facing and using smaller size straight needles, pick up 64 sts evenly spaced across Left Front edge including Neck Band.

Girl's: With **right** side facing and using smaller size straight needles, pick up 64 sts evenly spaced across Right Front edge including Neck Band.

Rows 1 and 2: (K1, P1) across.
Row 3 (Buttonhole row): K1, P1, K1, [YO, K2 tog **(buttonhole made)**], ★ (P1, K1) 6 times, YO, K2 tog; repeat from ★ 3 times **more**, P1, K1, P1: 5 buttonholes.
Rows 4 and 5: (K1, P1) across.

Bind off all sts in ribbing.

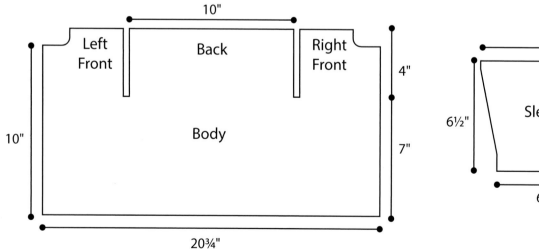

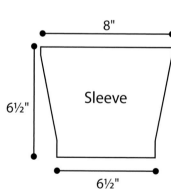

BUTTON BAND

With **right** side facing and using smaller size straight needles, pick up 64 sts evenly spaced across remaining Front edge including Neck Band.

Rows 1-5: (K1, P1) across.

Bind off all sts in ribbing.

Weave Sleeve seams *(Fig. 11, page 31)*.

Sew Sleeves to Sweater in armhole openings placing center of last row on Sleeves at shoulder seams.

Sew buttons to Button Band opposite buttonholes.

TIMELESS BLANKET

SHOPPING LIST

Yarn (Light Weight)

Peach Set

[5 ounces, 459 yards
(140 grams, 420 meters) per skein]:

☐ 5 skeins

Blue Set

[1.75 ounces, 161 yards
(50 grams, 147 meters) per skein]:

☐ 13 skeins

Knitting Needles

29" (73.5 cm) Circular,

☐ Size 5 (3.75 mm) **and**

☐ Size 7 (4.5 mm)

   or sizes needed for gauge

GAUGE INFORMATION

With larger size needle,

   in Body pattern and holding two
strands of yarn together,
18 sts and 18 rows = 3¾" (9.5 cm)

TECHNIQUES USED

- YO (*Fig. 1, page 30*)
- K2 tog (*Fig. 4, page 30*)
- K2 tog tbl (*Fig. 5, page 30*)
- Slip 2, K1, P2SSO (*Fig. 7, page 31*)

BOTTOM BORDER

With smaller size needle and holding
two strands of yarn together,
cast on 145 sts.

Rows 1-11: Knit across.

BODY

Change to larger size needle.

Row 1 (Right side)**:** K 10, K2 tog, YO,
K1, YO, K2 tog tbl, ★ K1, K2 tog, YO,
K1, YO, K2 tog tbl; repeat from ★
across to last 10 sts, K 10.

Row 2: K8, purl across to last 8 sts,
K8.

Row 3: K9, K2 tog, YO, K3, ★ YO,
slip 2, K1, P2SSO, YO, K3; repeat from
★ across to last 11 sts, YO, K2 tog tbl,
K9.

Row 4: K8, purl across to last 8 sts,
K8.

Row 5: K 10, YO, K2 tog tbl, K1,
K2 tog, ★ YO, K1, YO, K2 tog tbl, K1,
K2 tog; repeat from ★ across to last
10 sts, YO, K 10.

Row 6: K8, purl across to last 8 sts, K8.

Row 7: K 11, YO, slip 2, K1, P2SSO, ★ YO, K3, YO, slip 2, K1, P2SSO; repeat from ★ across to last 11 sts, YO, K 11.

Row 8: K8, purl across to last 8 sts, K8.

Repeat Rows 1-8 for pattern until piece measures approximately 43" (109 cm) from cast on edge, ending by working Row 8.

TOP BORDER

Change to smaller size needle.

Rows 1-11: Knit across.

Bind off all sts in **knit**.

DO THE TWIST SWEATER

Size: 6 months

Finished Chest Measurement: 22" (56 cm)

 INTERMEDIATE

SHOPPING LIST

Yarn (Light Weight)

[1.75 ounces, 161 yards (50 grams, 147 meters) per skein]:

☐ 3 skeins

Knitting Needles

29" (73.5 cm) Circular,

☐ Size 4 (3.5 mm) **and**

☐ Size 5 (3.75 mm)

 or sizes needed for gauge

Straight,

☐ Size 4 (3.5 mm) **and**

☐ Size 5 (3.75 mm)

 or sizes needed for gauge

Additional Supplies

☐ Point protectors - 2

☐ Stitch holders - 3

☐ Tapestry needle

☐ Sewing needle

☐ Sewing thread

☐ ⅝" (16 mm) buttons - 5

GAUGE INFORMATION

With larger size straight needles, in Body pattern,

16 sts and 20 rows = 2½" (6.25 cm)

TECHNIQUES USED

- YO (*Fig. 1, page 30*)
- Knit increase (*Figs. 2a & b, page 30*)
- Purl increase (*Fig. 3, page 30*)
- K2 tog (*Fig. 4, page 30*)
- SSK (*Figs. 6a-c, page 30*)

— STITCH GUIDE —

RIGHT TWIST (uses 2 sts)
Knit the second st on the left needle **(Fig. A)** making sure **not** to drop sts off, then knit the first st **(Fig. B)** letting both sts drop off the needle.

Fig. A

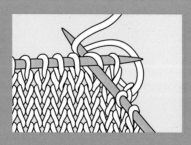

Fig. B

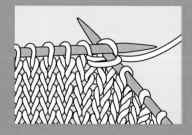

LEFT TWIST (uses 2 sts)
Working **behind** the first st on left needle, knit into the **back** of the second st **(Fig. C)** making sure **not** to drop off, then knit the first st **(Fig. D)** letting both sts drop off the needle.

Fig. C

Fig. D

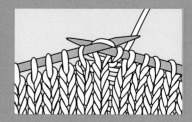

RIBBING

Sweater is worked in one piece to underarms.

With smaller size circular needle, cast on 136 sts.

Rows 1-7: (K1, P1) across.

BODY

Change to larger size circular needle.

Row 1 (Right side)**:** (Work Right Twist, work Left Twist) across.

Row 2: Purl across.

Row 3: Knit across.

Row 4: Purl across.

Row 5: (Work Left Twist, work Right Twist) across.

Row 6: Purl across.

Row 7: Knit across.

Row 8: Purl across.

Rows 9-48: Repeat Rows 1-8, 5 times.

Dividing Row: (Work Right Twist, work Left Twist) 7 times, K2, (Right Front), bind off next 7 sts (Armhole), (work Left Twist, work Right Twist) 15 times, K1 (Back), bind off next 7 sts (Armhole), K1, (work Right Twist, work Left Twist) across (Left Front): 30 sts on each Front and 62 sts on Back.

LEFT FRONT

Row 1: Using larger straight needles, purl across Left Front, leave remaining sts on circular needle and place point protectors on each end to keep sts from slipping off needle while working Left Front: 30 sts.

Row 2: Knit across.

Row 3: Purl across.

Row 4: Work Right Twist, (work Left Twist, work Right Twist) across.

Row 5: Purl across.

Row 6: Knit across.

Row 7: Purl across.

Row 8: Work Left Twist, (work Right Twist, work Left Twist) across.

Row 9: Purl across.

Rows 10-21: Repeat Rows 2-9 once, then repeat Rows 2-5 once **more**.

NECK SHAPING

Row 1: K 23, slip last 7 sts onto st holder.

Row 2: Purl across.

Row 3 (Decrease row)**:** (Work Left Twist, work Right Twist) across to last 3 sts, K2 tog, K1: 22 sts.

Row 4: Purl across.

Row 5 (Decrease row)**:** Knit across to last 3 sts, K2 tog, K1: 21 sts.

Row 6: Purl across.

Row 7 (Decrease row)**:** Work Right Twist, (work Left Twist, work Right Twist) across to last 3 sts, K2 tog, K1: 20 sts.

Row 8: Purl across.

Row 9: Knit across to last 3 sts, K2 tog, K1: 19 sts.

Rows 10-16: Repeat Rows 2-8: 16 sts.

Bind off remaining sts in **knit**, leaving a long end for sewing.

BACK

Row 1: With **wrong** side facing and using larger size straight needles, purl across Back, leave remaining sts on circular needle and place point protector on end to keep sts from slipping off needle while working Back: 62 sts.

Row 2: Knit across.

Row 3: Purl across.

Row 4: K1, (work Right Twist, work Left Twist) across to last st, K1.

Row 5: Purl across.

Row 6: Knit across.

Row 7: Purl across.

Row 8: K1, (work Left Twist, work Right Twist) across to last st, K1.

Row 9: Purl across.

Rows 10-37: Repeat Rows 2-9, 3 times; then repeat Rows 2-5 once **more**.

Rows 38 and 39: Bind off 16 sts, work across: 30 sts.

Slip remaining sts onto st holder.

RIGHT FRONT

Row 1: With **wrong** side facing and using larger size straight needles, purl across: 30 sts.

Row 2: Knit across.

Row 3: Purl across.

Row 4: Work Left Twist, (work Right Twist, work Left Twist) across.

Row 5: Purl across.

Row 6: Knit across.

Row 7: Purl across.

Row 8: Work Right Twist, (work Left Twist, work Right Twist) across.

Row 9: Purl across.

Rows 10-21: Repeat Rows 2-9 once, then repeat Rows 2-5 once **more**.

NECK SHAPING

Row 1: K7, slip 7 sts just worked onto st holder, knit across: 23 sts.

Row 2: Purl across.

Row 3 (Decrease row)**:** K1, SSK, (work Left Twist, work Right Twist) across: 22 sts.

Row 4: Purl across.

Row 5 (Decrease row)**:** K1, SSK, knit across: 21 sts.

Row 6: Purl across.

Row 7 (Decrease row)**:** K1, SSK, work Left Twist, (work Right Twist, work Left Twist) across: 20 sts.

Row 8: Purl across.

Row 9: K1, SSK, knit across: 19 sts.

Rows 10-16: Repeat Rows 2-8: 16 sts.

Bind off remaining sts in **knit**, leaving a long end for sewing.

SLEEVE (Make 2)
RIBBING

With smaller size straight needles, cast on 42 sts.

Rows 1-6: (K1, P1) across.

Row 7: Knit increase, (P1, K1) across to last st, purl increase: 44 sts.

BODY

Change to larger size straight needles.

Row 1 (Right side)**:** (Work Right Twist, work Left Twist) across.

Row 2: Purl across.

Row 3: Knit across.

Row 4: Purl across.

Row 5: (Work Left Twist, work Right Twist) across.

Row 6: Purl across.

Row 7 (Increase row)**:** Knit increase, knit across to last st, knit increase: 46 sts.

Row 8: Purl across.

Maintaining established pattern, continue to increase one stitch at **each** edge in same manner, every sixth row once, then increase every eighth row, 3 times: 54 sts.

Work even until Sleeve measures approximately 6½" (16.5 cm) from cast on edge, ending by working a **purl** row.

Bind off all sts in **knit**.

FINISHING

Sew shoulder seams.

NECK BAND

With **right** side facing and using smaller size straight needles, knit 7 sts from Right Front st holder, pick up 14 sts evenly spaced along Right Front neck edge *(Fig. 10, page 31)*, slip 30 sts from Back st holder onto empty needle and knit across, pick up 15 sts evenly spaced along Left Front neck edge, slip 7 sts from Left Front st holder onto empty needle and knit across: 73 sts.

Row 1: K1, (P1, K1) across.

Row 2: P1, (K1, P1) across.

Rows 3-5: Repeat Rows 1 and 2 once, then repeat Row 1 once **more**.

Bind off all sts in ribbing.

BUTTONHOLE BAND

Boy's: With **right** side facing and using smaller size straight needles, pick up 64 sts evenly spaced across Left Front edge including Neck Band.

Girl's: With **right** side facing and using smaller size straight needles, pick up 64 sts evenly spaced across Right Front edge including Neck Band.

Rows 1 and 2: (K1, P1) across.
Row 3 (Buttonhole row): K1, P1, K1, [YO, K2 tog (**buttonhole made**)], ★ (P1, K1) 6 times, YO, K2 tog; repeat from ★ 3 times **more**, P1, K1, P1: 5 buttonholes.
Rows 4 and 5: (K1, P1) across.

Bind off all sts in ribbing.

BUTTON BAND

With **right** side facing and using smaller size needle, pick up 64 sts evenly spaced across remaining Front edge including Neck Band.

Rows 1-5: (K1, P1) across.

Bind off all sts in ribbing.

Sew Sleeves to Sweater in armhole openings placing center of last row on Sleeves at shoulder seams.

Weave Sleeve seams (**Fig. 11, page 31**).

Sew buttons to Button Band opposite buttonholes.

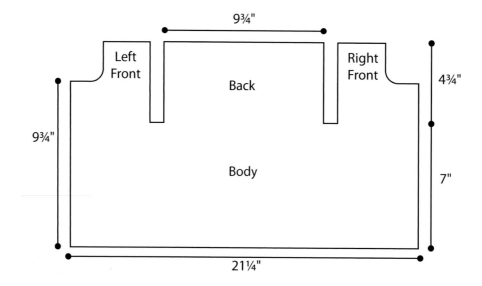

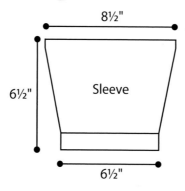

DO THE TWIST BLANKET

Finished Size:
31" x 37½"
(78.5 cm x 95.5 cm)
Shown on page 17.

 EASY

SHOPPING LIST

Yarn (Light Weight) 🧶 **3**

[1.75 ounces, 161 yards
(50 grams, 147 meters) per skein]:

☐ 12 skeins

Knitting Needles

29" (73.5 cm) Circular,

☐ Size 5 (3.75 mm) **and**

☐ Size 7 (4.5 mm)

   or sizes needed for gauge

GAUGE INFORMATION

In pattern,

   with larger size needle and

   holding two strands of yarn

   together,

   16 sts = 3¼" (8.25 cm);

   20 rows = 3" (7.5 cm)

—STITCH GUIDE—

RIGHT TWIST (uses 2 sts)
Knit the second st on
the left needle **(Fig. A,
page 16)** making sure
not to drop sts off, then
knit the first st **(Fig. B,
page 16)** letting both sts
drop off the needle.

LEFT TWIST (uses 2 sts)
Working **behind** the first
st on left needle, knit into
the **back** of the second
st **(Fig. C, page 16)**
making sure not to drop
sts off, then knit the first
st **(Fig. D, page 16)**
letting both sts drop off
the needle.

BOTTOM BORDER

With smaller size needle and
holding two strands of yarn
together, cast on 152 sts.

Rows 1-4: Knit across.

BODY

Change to larger size needle.

Row 1: K4, purl across to last 4 sts, K4.

Row 2 (Right side)**:** K4, (work Right Twist, work Left Twist) across to last 4 sts, K4.

Row 3: K4, purl across to last 4 sts, K4.

Row 4: Knit across.

Row 5: K4, purl across to last 4 sts, K4.

Row 6: K4, (work Left Twist, work Right Twist) across to last 4 sts, K4.

Row 7: K4, purl across to last 4 sts, K4.

Row 8: Knit across.

Repeat Rows 1-8 for pattern until piece measures approximately 37" (94 cm) from cast on edge, ending by working Row 7.

TOP BORDER

Change to smaller size needle.

Rows 1-4: Knit across.

Bind off all sts in **knit**.

21

COZY CABLES SWEATER

Size: 6 months

Finished Chest Measurement: 20½" (52 cm)

■■■□ INTERMEDIATE

SHOPPING LIST

Yarn (Light Weight)

[3.5 ounces, 359 yards
(100 grams, 328 meters) per skein]:

☐ 1 skein

Knitting Needles

29" (73.5 cm) Circular,

☐ Size 6 (4 mm)

or size needed for gauge

Straight,

☐ Size 6 (4 mm)

or size needed for gauge

Additional Supplies

☐ Cable needle

☐ Point protectors - 2

☐ Stitch holders - 3

☐ Tapestry needle

☐ Sewing needle

☐ Sewing thread

☐ ⁹⁄₁₆" (14 mm) buttons - 3

GAUGE INFORMATION

In Reverse Stockinette Stitch,
24 sts and 32 rows = 4" (10 cm)

TECHNIQUES USED

• YO (*Fig. 1, page 30*)

• Knit increase (*Figs. 2a & b, page 30*)

• Purl increase (*Fig. 3, page 30*)

• K2 tog (*Fig. 4, page 30*)

• SSK (*Figs. 6a-c, page 30*)

• P2 tog (*Fig. 8, page 31*)

• SSP (*Fig. 9, page 31*)

─ STITCH GUIDE ─

CABLE 6 FRONT
(abbreviated C6F)
(uses 6 sts)
Slip next 3 sts onto cable
needle and hold in front of
work, K3 from left needle,
K3 from cable needle.

CABLE 6 BACK
(abbreviated C6B)
(uses 6 sts)
Slip next 3 sts onto cable
needle and hold in back of
work, K3 from left needle,
K3 from cable needle.

BAND

Sweater is worked in one piece to underarms.

With circular needle, cast on 132 sts.

Rows 1-6: Knit across.

BODY

Row 1 (Right side): K4, P2, K6, purl across to last 12 sts, K6, P2, K4.

Row 2: P4, K2, P6, knit across to last 12 sts, P6, K2, P4.

Row 3: P6, K6, purl across to last 12 sts, K6, P6.

Row 4: P4, K2, P6, knit across to last 12 sts, P6, K2, P4.

Row 5: K4, P2, work C6F, purl across to last 12 sts, work C6B, P2, K4.

Row 6: K6, P6, knit across to last 12 sts, P6, K6.

Row 7: K4, P2, K6, purl across to last 12 sts, K6, P2, K4.

Row 8: P4, K2, P6, knit across to last 12 sts, P6, K2, P4.

Row 9: P6, K6, purl across to last 12 sts, K6, P6.

Row 10: P4, K2, P6, knit across to last 12 sts, P6, K2, P4.

Row 11: K4, P2, K6, purl across to last 12 sts, K6, P2, K4.

Row 12: K6, P6, knit across to last 12 sts, P6, K6.

Row 13: K4, P2, work C6F, purl across to last 12 sts, work C6B, P2, K4.

Row 14: P4, K2, P6, knit across to last 12 sts, P6, K2, P4.

Row 15: P6, K6, purl across to last 12 sts, K6, P6.

Row 16: P4, K2, P6, knit across to last 12 sts, P6, K2, P4.

Row 17: K4, P2, K6, purl across to last 12 sts, K6, P2, K4.

Row 18: K6, P6, knit across to last 12 sts, P6, K6.

Row 19: K4, P2, K6, purl across to last 12 sts, K6, P2, K4.

23

Row 20: P4, K2, P6, knit across to last 12 sts, P6, K2, P4.

Row 21: P6, work C6F, purl across to last 12 sts, work C6B, P6.

Row 22: P4, K2, P6, knit across to last 12 sts, P6, K2, P4.

Row 23: K4, P2, K6, purl across to last 12 sts, K6, P2, K4.

Row 24: K6, P6, knit across to last 12 sts, P6, K6.

Rows 25-48: Repeat Rows 1-24.

Dividing Row: K2, [YO, K2 tog (buttonhole made)], P2, K6, P 19, (Right Front), bind off next 6 sts (Armhole), P 57, bind off next 6 sts (Armhole), P 18, K6, P2, K4 (Left Front): 31 sts on **each** Front and 58 sts on Back.

LEFT FRONT
ARMHOLE SHAPING

Row 1: Using straight needles, P4, K2, P6, knit across Left Front, leave remaining sts on circular needle and place point protectors on each end to keep sts from slipping off needle while working Left Front: 31 sts.

Row 2: P1, SSP, P 16, K6, P6: 30 sts.

Row 3: P4, K2, P6, knit across.

Row 4: P1, SSP, P 15, work C6B, P2, K4: 29 sts.

Row 5: K6, P6, knit across.

Row 6: P1, SSP, P 14, K6, P2, K4: 28 sts.

Row 7: P4, K2, P6, knit across.

Row 8: P 16, K6, P6.

Row 9: P4, K2, P6, knit across.

Row 10: P 16, K6, P2, K4.

Row 11: K6, P6, knit across.

Row 12: P 16, work C6B, P2, K4.

Rows 13-17: Repeat Rows 7-11.

Row 18: P 16, K6, P2, K4.

Row 19: P4, K2, P6, knit across.

NECK SHAPING

Row 1: P 16, K2, slip last 10 sts onto st holder: 18 sts.

Row 2: P2, K 16.

Row 3: Purl across to last 3 sts, P2 tog, K1: 17 sts.

Row 4: P1, knit across.

Row 5 (Decrease row)**:** Purl across to last 3 sts, P2 tog, P1: 16 sts.

Row 6: Knit across.

Rows 7-12: Repeat Rows 5 and 6, 3 times: 13 sts.

Bind off all sts in **purl**, leaving a long end for sewing.

BACK
ARMHOLE SHAPING

Row 1: With **wrong** facing and using straight needles, knit across Back, leave remaining sts on circular needle and place point protector on end to keep sts from slipping off needle while working Back.

Row 2 (Decrease row)**:** P1, SSP, purl across to last 3 sts, P2 tog, P1: 56 sts.

Row 3: Knit across.

Rows 4-6: Repeat Rows 2 and 3 once, then repeat Row 2 once **more**: 52 sts.

Work even in Reverse Stockinette Stitch until Back measures same as Left Front, ending by working a **knit** row.

Last 2 Rows: Bind off 13 sts, work across: 26 sts.

Slip remaining sts onto st holder.

RIGHT FRONT
ARMHOLE SHAPING

Row 1: With **wrong** side facing and using straight needles, K 19, P6, K2, P4.

Row 2: P6, K6, purl across to last 3 sts, P2 tog, P1: 30 sts.

Row 3: K 18, P6, K2, P4.

Row 4: K4, P2, work C6F, purl across to last 3 sts, P2 tog, P1: 29 sts.

Row 5: K 17, P6, K6.

Row 6: K4, P2, K6, purl across to last 3 sts, P2 tog, P1: 28 sts.

Row 7: K 16, P6, K2, P4.

Row 8: P6, K6, purl across.

Row 9: K 16, P6, K2, P4.

Row 10: K4, P2, K6, purl across.

Row 11: K 16, P6, K6.

Row 12 (Buttonhole row)**:** K2, **[**YO, K2 tog **(buttonhole made)]**, P2, work C6F, purl across.

Rows 13-17: Repeat Rows 7-11.

Row 18: K4, P2, K6, purl across.

Row 19: K 16, P6, K2, P4.

NECK SHAPING

Row 1: P6, K4, slip 10 sts just worked onto st holder, K2, purl across: 18 sts.

Row 2: K 16, P2.

Row 3: K1, SSP, purl across: 17 sts.

Row 4: Knit across to last st, P1.

Row 5 (Decrease row)**:** P1, SSP, purl across: 16 sts.

Row 6: Knit across.

Rows 7-12: Repeat Rows 5 and 6, 3 times: 13 sts.

Bind off all sts in **purl**, leaving a long end for sewing.

RIGHT SLEEVE
BAND

With straight needles, cast on 34 sts.

Rows 1-5: Knit across.

Row 6: Knit increase, knit across to last st, knit increase: 36 sts.

BODY

Row 1 (Right side): P 15, K6, P 15.

Row 2: K 15, P6, K 15.

Rows 3 and 4: Repeat Rows 1 and 2.

Row 5: P 15, work C6F, P 15.

Row 6: K 15, P6, K 15.

Row 7: P 15, K6, P 15.

Rows 8-10: Repeat Rows 6 and 7 once, then repeat Row 6 once **more**.

Row 11: Purl increase, P 14, K6, P 14, purl increase: 38 sts.

Row 12: K 16, P6, K 16.

Row 13: P 16, work C6F, P 16.

Row 14: K 16, P6, K 16.

Row 15: P 16, K6, P 16.

Rows 16-20: Repeat Rows 14 and 15 twice, then repeat Row 14 once **more**.

Row 21: P 16, work C6F, P 16.

Row 22: K 16, P6, K 16.

Row 23: Purl increase, P 15, K6, P 15, purl increase: 40 sts.

Row 24: K 17, P6, K 17.

Row 25: P 17, K6, P 17.

Rows 26-28: Repeat Rows 24 and 25 once, then repeat Row 24 once **more**.

Row 29: P 17, work C6F, P 17.

Rows 30-34: Repeat Rows 24-28.

Row 35: Purl increase, P 16, K6, P 16, purl increase: 42 sts.

Row 36: K 18, P6, K 18.

Row 37: P 18, work C6F, P 18.

Row 38: K 18, P6, K 18.

Row 39: P 18, K6, P 18.

Rows 40-44: Repeat Rows 38 and 39 twice, then repeat Row 38 once **more**.

CAP SHAPING

Maintain established pattern throughout.

Rows 1 and 2: Bind off 3 sts, work across: 36 sts.

Row 3 (Decrease row): P1, SSP, work across to last 3 sts, P2 tog, P1: 34 sts.

Row 4: Work across.

Rows 5-9: Repeat Rows 3 and 4 twice, then repeat Row 3 once **more**: 28 sts.

Rows 10-12: Work across.

Row 13 (Decrease row): P1, SSP, work across to last 3 sts, P2 tog, P1: 26 sts.

Rows 14-25: Repeat Rows 10-13, 3 times: 20 sts.

Row 26: Work across.

Rows 27 and 28: Bind off 4 sts, work across: 12 sts.

Bind off remaining sts in **purl**.

LEFT SLEEVE

Work same as Right Sleeve, substituting C6F with C6B.

FINISHING

Sew shoulder seams.

NECK BAND

With **right** side facing and using straight needles, knit 10 sts from Right Front st holder, pick up 9 sts evenly spaced along Right Front neck edge *(Fig. 10, page 31)*, slip 26 sts from Back st holder onto empty needle and knit across, pick up 9 sts evenly spaced along Left Front neck edge, slip 10 sts from Left Front st holder onto empty needle and knit across: 64 sts.

Rows 1-3: Knit across.

Row 4 (Buttonhole row): K2, **[**YO, K2 tog (**buttonhole made)]**, knit across.

Rows 5-7: Knit across.

COLLAR

Row 1: Bind off 4 sts, K3, purl across to last 8 sts, K8: 60 sts.

Row 2: Bind off 4 sts, K3, knit increase, (K2, knit increase) across to last 3 sts, K3: 73 sts.

Row 3: K4, purl across to last 4 sts, K4.

Row 4: Knit across.

Row 5: K4, purl across to last 4 sts, K4.

Row 6: K4, knit increase, (K2, knit increase) across to last 8 sts, K3, knit increase, K4: 95 sts.

Row 7: K4, purl across to last 4 sts, K4.

Row 8: Knit across.

Row 9: K4, purl across to last 4 sts, K4.

Rows 10-14: Knit across.

Bind off all sts in **knit**.

Sew Sleeves to Sweater, placing center of last row on Sleeve Cap at shoulder seam and matching bound off stitches.

Weave Sleeve seams *(Fig. 11, page 31)*.

Sew buttons to Left Front opposite buttonholes.

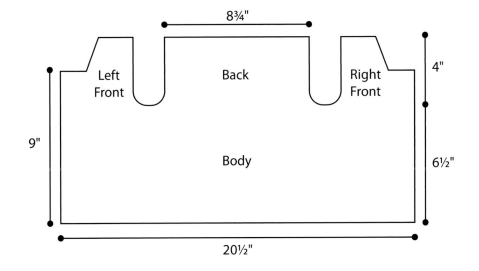

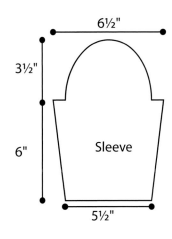

COZY CABLES BLANKET

Finished Size:
32" x 45"
(81.5 cm x 114.5 cm)

■□□□□ **EASY**

SHOPPING LIST

Yarn (Light Weight)

[3.5 ounces, 359 yards
(100 grams, 328 meters) per skein]:

☐ 8 skeins

Knitting Needles

29" (73.5 cm) Circular,

☐ Size 5 (3.75 mm) **and**

☐ Size 7 (4.5 mm)

or sizes needed for gauge

Additional Supplies

☐ Cable needle

GAUGE INFORMATION

With larger size needle,
in Reverse Stockinette Stitch and
holding two strands of yarn
together,
18 sts and 28 rows = 4" (10 cm)

— STITCH GUIDE —

CABLE 6 FRONT
(abbreviated C6B)
(uses 6 sts)
Slip 3 sts onto cable needle
and hold in front of work,
K3 from left needle, K3
from cable needle.

BOTTOM BORDER

With smaller size needle and holding
two strands of yarn together,
cast on 180 sts.

Rows 1-8: Knit across.

BODY

Change to larger size needle.

Row 1 (Right side)**:** K 10, P5, K6, (P 10,
K6) 9 times, P5, K 10.

Row 2: K 15, P6, (K 10, P6) 9 times,
K 15.

Rows 3 and 4: Repeat Rows 1 and 2.

Row 5: K 10, P5, work C6F, (P 10, work
C6F) 9 times, P5, K 10.

Row 6: K 15, P6, (K 10, P6) 9 times,
K 15.

Row 7: K 10, P5, K6, (P 10, K6) 9 times,
P5, K 10.

Rows 8-12: Repeat Rows 6 and 7
twice, then repeat Row 6 once **more**.

Repeat Rows 5-12 for pattern until
piece measures approximately 44¼"
(112.5 cm) from cast on edge, ending
by working Row 8.

TOP BORDER

Change to smaller size needle.

Rows 1-8: Knit across.

Bind off all sts in **knit**.

GENERAL INSTRUCTIONS

ABBREVIATIONS

	Cable 6 Back
	Cable 6 Front
	centimeters
	knit
mm	millimeters
P	purl
P2SSO	pass 2 slipped stitches over
SSK	slip, slip, knit
SSP	slip, slip, purl
st(s)	stitch(es)
tbl	through back loop(s)
tog	together
YO	yarn over

SYMBOLS & TERMS

★ — work instructions following ★ as many **more** times as indicated in addition to the first time.

( ) or **[ ]** — work enclosed instructions **as many** times as specified by the number immediately following **or** contains explanatory remarks.

colon (:) — the number(s) given after a colon at the end of a row denote(s) the number of stitches you should have on that row.

work even — work without increasing or decreasing in the established pattern.

GAUGE

Exact gauge is **essential** for proper fit. Before beginning your project, make a sample swatch in the yarn and needle specified in the individual instructions. After completing the swatch, measure it, counting your stitches and rows carefully. If your swatch is larger or smaller than specified, **make another, changing needle size to get the correct gauge**. Keep trying until you find the size needles that will give you the specified gauge.

KNIT TERMINOLOGY	
UNITED STATES	**INTERNATIONAL**
gauge =	tension
bind off =	cast off
yarn over (YO) =	yarn forward (yfwd) **or** yarn around needle (yrn)

Yarn Weight Symbol & Names	LACE 0	SUPER FINE 1	FINE 2	LIGHT 3	MEDIUM 4	BULKY 5	SUPER BULKY 6	JUMBO 7
Type of Yarns in Category	Fingering, size 10 crochet thread	Sock, Fingering, Baby	Sport, Baby	DK, Light Worsted	Worsted, Afghan, Aran	Chunky, Craft, Rug	Super Bulky, Roving	Jumbo, Roving
Knit Gauge Ranges in Stockinette St to 4" (10 cm)	33-40 sts**	27-32 sts	23-26 sts	21-24 sts	16-20 sts	12-15 sts	7-11 sts	6 sts and fewer
Advised Needle Size Range	000 to 1	1 to 3	3 to 5	5 to 7	7 to 9	9 to11	11 to 17	17 and larger

* GUIDELINES ONLY: The chart above reflects the most commonly used gauges and needle sizes for specific yarn categories.

** Lace weight yarns are usually knitted on larger needles to create lacy openwork patterns. Accordingly, a gauge range is difficult to determine. Always follow the gauge stated in your pattern.

▬▭▭▭ **BEGINNER**	Projects for first-time knitters using basic knit and purl stitches. Minimal shaping.
▬▬▭▭ **EASY**	Projects using basic stitches, repetitive stitch patterns, simple color changes, and simple shaping and finishing.
▬▬▬▭ **INTERMEDIATE**	Projects with a variety of stitches, such as basic cables and lace, simple intarsia, double-pointed needles and knitting in the round needle techniques, mid-level shaping and finishing.
▬▬▬▬ **EXPERIENCED**	Projects using advanced techniques and stitches, such as short rows, fair isle, more intricate intarsia, cables, lace patterns, and numerous color changes.

KNITTING NEEDLES																		
U.S.	0	1	2	3	4	5	6	7	8	9	10	10½	11	13	15	17	19	35	50
U.K.	13	12	11	10	9	8	7	6	5	4	3	2	1	00	000	---	---	---	---
Metric - mm	2	2.25	2.75	3.25	3.5	3.75	4	4.5	5	5.5	6	6.5	8	9	10	12.75	15	19	25

YARN OVER
(abbreviated YO)

Bring the yarn forward **between** the needles, then back **over** the top of the right needle, so that it is now in position to knit the next stitch *(Fig. 1)*.

Fig. 1

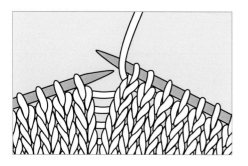

INCREASES
KNIT INCREASE

Knit the next stitch but do **not** slip the old stitch off the left needle *(Fig. 2a)*. Insert the right needle into the **back** loop of the **same** stitch and knit it *(Fig. 2b)*, then slip the old stitch off the left needle.

Fig. 2a   Fig. 2b

PURL INCREASE

Purl the next stitch but do **not** slip the old stitch off the left needle. Insert the right needle into the **back** loop of the **same** stitch from **back** to **front** and purl it. *(Fig. 3)*, then slip the old stitch off the left needle.

Fig. 3

DECREASES
KNIT 2 TOGETHER
(abbreviated K2 tog)

Insert the right needle into the **front** of the first two stitches on the left needle as if to **knit** *(Fig. 4)*, then **knit** them together as if they were one stitch.

Fig. 4

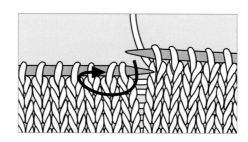

KNIT 2 TOGETHER
THROUGH BACK LOOP
(abbreviated K2 tog tbl)

Insert the right needle into the **back** of first two stitches on the left needle from **front** to **back** *(Fig. 5)*, then **knit** them together as if they were one stitch.

Fig. 5

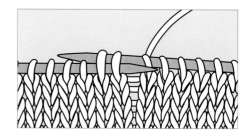

SLIP, SLIP, KNIT
(abbreviated SSK)

Separately slip two stitches as if to **knit** *(Fig. 6a)*. Insert the **left** needle into the **front** of both slipped stitches *(Fig. 6b)* and then **knit** them together as if they were one stitch *(Fig. 6c)*.

Fig. 6a   Fig. 6b

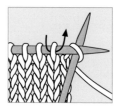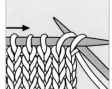

Fig. 6c

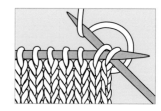

...P 2 AS IF TO KNIT, ...T 1, PASS 2 SLIPPED ...CHES OVER

...breviated slip 2, K1, P2SSO)

...rately slip two stitches as if to
...(Fig. 6a, page 32), then knit
... next stitch. With the left needle,
...ring both slipped stitches over the
knit stitch (Fig. 7) and off the needle.

Fig. 7

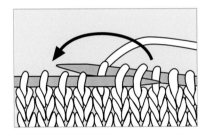

PURL 2 TOGETHER

(abbreviated P2 tog)

Insert the right needle into the **front**
of the first two stitches on the left
needle as if to **purl** (Fig. 8), then
purl them together as if they were
one stitch.

Fig. 8

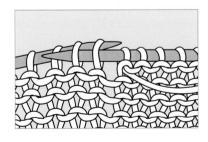

SLIP, SLIP, PURL

(abbreviated SSP)

Separately slip two stitches as if
to **knit** (Fig. 6a). Place these two
stitches back onto the left needle.
Insert the right needle into the **back**
of both stitches from **back** to **front**
(Fig. 9) and purl them together as if
they were one stitch.

Fig. 9

PICKING UP STITCHES

When instructed to pick up stitches,
insert the needle from **front** to **back**
under two strands at the edge of the
worked piece (Fig. 10). Put the yarn
around the needle as if to **knit**, then
bring the needle with the yarn back
through the stitch to the right side,
resulting in a stitch on the needle.
Repeat this along the edge, picking
up the required number of stitches.
A crochet hook may be helpful to
pull yarn through.

Fig. 10

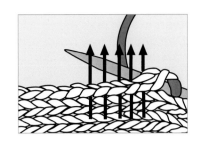

WEAVING SEAMS

With the **right** side of both pieces
facing you and edges even, sew
through both sides once to secure
the beginning of the the seam.
Insert the needle under the bar
between the first and second
stitches on the row and pull the yarn
through (Fig. 11). Insert the needle
under the next bar on the second
side. Repeat from side to side, being
careful to match rows. If the edges
are different lengths, it may be
necessary to insert the needle under
two bars at one edge.

Fig. 11

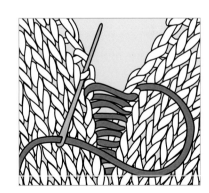

YARN INFORMATION

The items in this book were made using Light Weight Yarn. Any brand of Light Weight Yarn may be used. It is best to refer to the yardage/meters when determining how many balls or skeins to purchase. Remember, to arrive at the finished size, it is the GAUGE/TENSION that is important, not the brand of yarn.

For your convenience, listed below are specific yarns used to create our photography models. Because yarn manufacturers make frequent changes in their product lines, you may sometimes find it necessary to use a substitute yarn or to search for the discontinued product at alternate suppliers (locally or online).

SOFT TOUCH

Bernat® Softee® Baby™

#30205 Prettiest Pink

TIMELESS

Lion Brand® Babysoft®

Peach Set - #133 Creamsicle

Patons® Astra™

Blue Set - #02774 Medium Blue

DO THE TWIST

Patons® Astra™

#08737 Ocean Mist

COZY CABLES

Patons® Beehive Baby Sport™

#09309 Violet Mist

We have made every effort to ensure that these instructions are accurate and complete. We cannot, however, be responsible for human error, typographical mistakes, or variations in individual work.

The blue version of Timeless made and instructions tested by Margaret Taverner.

Production Team: Instructional/Technical Editor - Lois J. Long; Editorial Writer - Susan Frantz Wiles; Senior Graphic Artist - Lora Puls; Graphic Artist - Victoria Temple; Photo Stylist - Lori Wenger; and Photographer - Jason Masters.

Made in U.S.A.

MEET STARLA KRAMER

Starla Kramer is a lifelong knitter who enjoys making quick and simple projects, as well as long-term complex projects. She especially loves knitting baby gifts.

"Not a day goes by that I don't pick up a set of knitting needles," she says. "I believe anyone can knit if there's something you can find that you love and want to see on yourself or on someone else."

She says knitting "teaches you patience with yourself, and it's extremely rewarding when you've completed the project."

An Air Force veteran, Starla lives in Tennessee with her husband, three dogs, and six chickens. More of her designs may be found in *Dishcloths Made with the Knook* (Leisure Arts #5585).